THOUGHTFULNESS THINKING
Self-Control
AF575715
Vicky Bureau
M.S., School Counseling
A Starfish Book
SEAHORSE
PUBLISHING

Teaching Tips for Caregivers:

As a caregiver, you can help your child succeed in school by giving them a strong foundation in language and literacy skills and a desire to learn to read.

This book helps children grow by letting them practice reading skills.

Reading for pleasure and interest will help your child to develop reading skills and will give your child the opportunity to practice these skills in meaningful ways.

- Encourage your child to read on her own at home
- Encourage your child to practice reading aloud
- Encourage activities that require reading
- Establish a reading time
- Talk with your child
- Give your child writing materials

Teaching Tips for Teachers:

Research shows that one of the best ways for students to learn a new topic is to read about it.

Before Reading

- Read the "Words to Know" and discuss the meaning of each word.
- Read the back cover to see what the book is about.

During Reading

- When a student gets to a word that is unknown, ask them to look at the rest of the sentence to find clues to help with the meaning of the unknown word.
- Ask the student to write down any pages of the book that were confusing to them.

After Reading

- Discuss the main idea of the book.
- Ask students to give one detail that they learned in the book by showing a text dependent answer from the book.

TABLE OF CONTENTS

Self-Control: Do You Have It?

Are cartwheels for the cafeteria?

Do tadpoles belong in the bathtub?

Do you follow the rules at home and in school?

Or does your day end in TIME'S UP! and TIME OUT!?

Sometimes, it's hard to do the right thing.

We want to giggle and jiggle.

Or dilly and dally.

But having **self-control** means that we can stop and think.

Did you know that everyone makes mistakes?

Our mistakes help us learn.

They teach us about what we should do and what we should not do.

In other words, we all get mad. We've all been bored. And we've all felt scared.

But these emotions can sometimes cause us to lose self-control.

Self-Control: What Does It Mean?

Have you ever lost your self-control?

Have you ever made someone else feel sad because you did something when you were mad?

Self-control means being able to stop and think before you act. It means that you can use your experiences to help shape your **behaviors**.

Sometimes, it’s really hard to keep self-control.

Like when Tommy Zucchini slips worms into your desk. EWWW!

Or when Grandma makes you finish all your brussels sprouts. YUCK!

When you lose it, self-control doesn't hide under your bed or at the bottom of your backpack.

It's not something you can pick up, or even touch.

But finding and keeping self-control helps you make good decisions, be **kind**, and act **responsibly**.

It's not always easy, but it's always worth it. Because YOU are worth it!

Self-Control: How Can You Build Yours?

You can learn more about yourself! Want to know how?

Stop and think! Should I do this? Should I really say that?

How am I feeling right now? And how does that affect my behavior?

What Would You Do?

You have a funny joke to tell, but it's quiet reading time in class. Do you tell it anyway, or save it for recess?

You can't solve a math problem. Do you crumple the paper and give up, or ask a friend for help?

Let's review your answers!

Telling a new joke is so much fun! But understanding the difference between fun time and learning time helps you build a good **attitude** about school.

Trying new things can be frustrating. But having self-control helps you stay calm and keep trying, which builds **confidence**!

Words to Know

attitude (AT-i-tood): a person's way of thinking or feeling

behaviors (bi-HAYV-yurz): ways that you act, respond, and behave

confidence (KAHN-fuh-dens): a belief that you can succeed

kind (kighnd): wanting to do good and bring happiness

responsibly (ri-SPAHN-suh-blee): acting in a way that shows you understand the rules and choose to follow them

self-control (self kuhn-TROHL): being able to manage your thoughts and actions

Index

Comprehension Questions

1. How can you show self-control even when things seem hard or difficult?

2. What are some things you can do to help build self-control?

3. How does a person's self-control affect their behavior?

4. What does it mean to have self-control?

5. What happens when you lose self-control? How can you find it?

About the Author

Vicky Bureau was born in Longueuil, Quebec, and was raised in South Florida. As a teacher, she developed a passion for the social and emotional growth of her students and later transitioned into the area of child and adolescent psychology after earning her master's degree in school counseling. In addition to working with children, Vicky loves to be surrounded by animals and nature. She lives in Fort Lauderdale with her family: Billy, Khloe, M.J., and Max; her three cats, Alley, Baguette, and Salem; and her dog, Boomer.

Written by: Vicky Bureau
Design by: Under the Oaks Media
Editor: Kim Thompson

Photographs/Shutterstock: Benjavisa Rvangvaree: cover, p. 1; Sakda Narathipwan: p. 4; Roman Chazov: p. 5; Robert Kneschke: p. 6; Purino: p. 7; Zurijeta: p. 8; Rido: p. 9; ESBProfessional: p. 10; Rusiana Iurchenko: p. 11; brewing thought: p. 13; Carlos Horta: p. 15; Nareluya: p. 16a; wavebreakmedia: p. 18=6b; Prostock Studio: p. 17a; Monkey Business Images: p. 17b; Millat: p. 19

Library of Congress PCN Data
Self-Control / Vicky Bureau
Thoughtfulness Thinking
ISBN 978-1-63897-095-8 (hard cover)
ISBN 978-1-63897-181-8 (paperback)
ISBN 978-1-63897-267-9 (EPUB)
ISBN 978-1-63897-353-9 (eBook)
Library of Congress Control Number: 2021945243

Printed in the United States of America.

Seahorse Publishing Company
www.seahorsepub.com

Published in the United States
Seahorse Publishing
PO Box 771325
Coral Springs, FL 33077